An
Exercises Accompanying

THE
BRIEF HOLT
HANDBOOK

Second Edition
KIRSZNER & MANDELL

Answer Key to the Exercises Accompanying

THE *BRIEF* HOLT HANDBOOK

Second Edition
KIRSZNER & MANDELL

Prepared by

Scott Douglass
Chattanooga
State Technical
Community College

Peggy B. Jolly
University of
Alabama
at Birmingham

Judy A. Pearce
Montgomery
College

Harcourt Brace College Publishers

Fort Worth   Philadelphia   San Diego
New York   Orlando   Austin   San Antonio
Toronto   Montreal   London   Sydney   Tokyo

ISBN: 0-15-508263-9

Copyright © 1998, 1995 by Harcourt Brace & Company

All rights reserved. No part of this publication may be reproduced or transmitted in any form or by any means, electronic or mechanical, including photocopy, recording, or any information storage and retrieval system, without permission in writing from the publisher.

Requests for permission to make copies of any part of the work should be mailed to: Permissions Department, Harcourt Brace & Company, 6277 Sea Harbor Drive, Orlando, Florida 32887-6777.

Address editorial correspondence to:
Harcourt Brace College Publishers
301 Commerce Street, Suite 3700
Fort Worth, TX 76102

Address orders to:
Harcourt Brace & Company
6277 Sea Harbor Drive
Orlando, FL 32887
1-800-782-4479 outside Florida
1-800-433-0001 inside Florida

Printed in the United States of America

7 8 9 0 1 2 3 4 5 6   023   9 8 7 6 5 4 3 2 1

Answers to Exercise 1: Getting Started

Answers will vary. The following considerations should be raised in discussion:

Journal entry: content likely to be a personal response to the book rather than an analysis of content; style very informal; organization probably not evident; tone judgmental, depending on student's reaction to book: emphasis on personal response and specific details.

Examination question: content concerned mainly with summarizing material in book; style formal; careful organization, probably following that of book; tone neutral, nonjudgmental; emphasis on providing information about book's content.

Book review: content an evaluation of book's material and presentation; style formal; organization formal, probably presenting book's strengths and weaknesses in an orderly manner; tone neutral; emphasis on balance of evaluation.

Letter to school board: content likely to be persuasive reasons not to ban books in general, with or without acknowledging faults of this particular book; style formal, given large, mostly unknown audience; careful organization, probably with a hierarchy of reasons not to ban book; tone committed, but not overly emotional; emphasis probably on importance of free access to books.

Editorial for newspaper: content probably reasons not to read the book; style somewhat less formal, given audience of student peers; organization probably less formal, but orderly; tone likely to be committed and, because of shared assumptions of audience, probably more emotional; emphasis on book's lack of value.

Answers to Exercise 2: Considering Purpose and Audience

Answers will vary. For this exercise, assign or have students choose a subject that can be developed into the first essay of the term.

Answers to Exercise 3: Listing

Answers will vary. You might wish to do your own list to stimulate discussion and to provide another perspective as you talk about discovering a topic and planning a paper.

Answers to Exercise 4: Freewriting

Answers will vary.

ANSWERS TO EXERCISE 5: BRAINSTORMING

Answers will vary.

ANSWERS TO EXERCISE 6: JOURNAL ENTRY

Answers will vary.

ANSWERS TO EXERCISE 7: CLUSTER DIAGRAM/TOPIC TREE

Answers will vary. A student's first attempts at a cluster diagram or a topic tree may not be extremely well developed, but with practice, your students should improve.

ANSWERS TO EXERCISE 8: DEVELOPING A THESIS

1. An announcement, not a thesis.
2. A subject, not a thesis. Gives no indication of essay's focus or direction, let alone writer's position.
3. A subject, not a thesis. Why should it be avoided? What coast? What kind of development? What constitutes overdevelopment?
4. No position indicated. What aspects will be considered? What pattern of development might be used? What standards of judgment will be used?
5. A good start, but "but it has some disadvantages" is not specific enough.
6. A subject, not a thesis. What position? Do all environmentalists share a single position?
7. States a fact.
8. A good start, but needs clearer focus. Thesis is too general.
9. States a fact.
10. States a personal opinion. Question of taste. Hard to develop objectively or concretely.

ANSWERS TO EXERCISE 9: STATING A THESIS

Answers will vary.

1. A husband can profoundly influence his wife by determining the location where they live, their social status, and their circle of friends.
2. The Second Amendment, which provides for individual ownership of firearms, comes into direct conflict with the proponents of gun control.

3. Although California and Arizona recently voted to allow the medical use of marijuana, this decision has been challenged by the federal government.
4. The concerns over the viability of the social security system have caused Baby Boomers and younger generations to rethink the use of a multitude of savings vehicles for their retirement.
5. In addition to increased potential earning power, a college education offers many intangible benefits.
6. Public funding of the arts has been criticized because many believe they should be self supporting or privately funded.
7. Many shoplifters attempt to justify their actions as a simple redistribution of material wealth.
8. Cultural diversity has different meanings for many people.
9. The breakdown of discipline and the diminishing educational standards have caused many parents to prefer parochial rather than secular schools.
10. Although the First Amendment guarantees freedom of speech, political correctness often inhibits its exercise.

ANSWERS TO EXERCISE 10: STATING A THESIS

Although answers will vary, the following thesis statements might reasonably be derived from the material:

Whereas humans practice warfare extensively with the intent to kill, most other animal species engage in destructive combat as a means to maintain stable population densities in the wild.

Although male animals in the wild sometimes engage in battle to establish dominance, leading to the "Nature, red in tooth and claw" legend, most ritualistic destructive combat with the intent to kill is reserved for maintaining stable population densities.

The "Nature, red in tooth and claw" legend is played out in most animal species through automatic and ritualistic mechanisms that help to maintain stable population densities in the wild and to establish dominance.

ANSWERS TO EXERCISE 11: THESIS

Answers will vary.

ANSWERS TO EXERCISE 12: INFORMAL OUTLINE

Answers will vary. Small-group discussions of informal outlines may be a good classroom exercise.

ANSWERS TO EXERCISE 13: ROUGH DRAFT

Encourage students to use the prewriting exercises they have just completed to guide their writing.

ANSWERS TO EXERCISE 14: COLLABORATIVE REVISION

Answers will vary. You might want to circulate among the teams to encourage constructive peer reviews, particularly if students are collaborating for the first time.

ANSWERS TO EXERCISE 15: CUSTOMIZED CHECKLIST

At first, students may need your help to distinguish between the concerns of revision and those of editing.

ANSWERS TO EXERCISE 16: CENTRAL IDEA—TOPIC SENTENCE

Answers will vary.

A. Unifying idea: Themes of Ralph Ellison's novel *Invisible Man*

   Topic sentence: In *Invisible Man* Ralph Ellison is concerned at least as much with self-discovery as he is with race relations. (This sentence could be placed at either the beginning or the end of the paragraph.)

B. Unifying idea: Problems in food labeling

   Topic sentence: Food labels have recently begun to give consumers a great deal of nutritional information, but too often this information is difficult to decipher. (Make this the first sentence in the paragraph.)

ANSWERS TO EXERCISE 17: COHERENCE WITHIN PARAGRAPHS

A. Answers will vary, as individual perceptions of coherence will lead students to different conclusions. Certainly they should notice the obvious links, such as parallel elements in the first sentence, the repetition of the words *pigeons* and *El*, and the repetition of the pronoun *they*.

B. The theory of continental drift was first put forward by Alfred Wegener in 1912. *He believed that* the continents fit together like a giant jigsaw puzzle. *Because* the opposing Atlantic coasts, especially those of South America and Africa, seem to have been attached, *he also believed that* at one time, probably 225 million years ago, there was one supercontinent *which* broke into parts that eventually drifted into their present positions. The theory, *which* stirred controversy during the 1920s, eventually was ridiculed by the scientific community. *However, the theory of continental drift* was revived in 1954 and is now accepted as a reasonable geological explanation of the continental system.

ANSWERS TO EXERCISE 18: COHERENCE AMONG PARAGRAPHS

Answers will vary. The simplest way to improve the coherence of these paragraphs is probably to use transitional expressions at the beginning of each new paragraph: "In the 1970s *The Brady Bunch* featured six children . . . ." and "More recently, *The Cosby Show* was extremely popular . . . ."

ANSWERS TO EXERCISE 19:
PATTERNS OF PARAGRAPH DEVELOPMENT

1. definition, description
2. process analysis
3. classification
4. description, definition
5. comparison and contrast
6. cause and effect
7. exemplification, description
8. process analysis, narration
9. argument, exemplification
10. cause and effect, exemplification

ANSWERS TO EXERCISE 20: WELL-DEVELOPED PARAGRAPHS

1. The paragraph could be further developed by exemplification, giving additional examples of how breaches of civility are settled in our society. Lawsuits, gang violence, or physical abuse in close relationships may be included as methods of how people attempt to settle their differences.

2. This paragraph could be further developed by enumeration of amounts of specific ingredients, types of containers, and utensils used. Baking times and temperatures can vary. Methods of storing and preserving the batter could be included. Flavoring and leavening are important ingredients to be discussed. Generally accepted bread-making procedures could be used as a guide for completing the process.
3. The paragraph could be further developed by describing characteristics that connote the Liberal, Conservative, and Silent Majority's viewpoints. Examples of programs or policies attributed to each group could also be included.
4. The paragraph could be developed by using characteristics of comparison and contrast. Either point-by-point or subject-by-subject development is acceptable. Supporting details such as description of vacation place, budgeting considerations, and time available are appropriate methods of development.
5. The paragraph could be developed using process analysis. It is important that the student present the steps of the planning process completely and in order. Students should remember to include appropriate warnings that will guide the reader to avoid issues that could undermine the effectiveness of the gathering.
6. The paragraph could be developed as an argument. If the student chooses to use the classical form of development, development will include *ethos*, the authority of the author, *pathos*, emotional manipulation, and *logos*, rational evidence. If the student chooses to use Toulmin's form of argument, *warrants* and *evidence* should be identified. In either type of development, the student should include both sides of the argument rather than just the one he or she favors.

ANSWERS TO EXERCISE 21: REVISING SENTENCE FRAGMENTS

Muscle cars were introduced to Americans in the 1960s, when the price of gasoline was relatively inexpensive. The cars evolved from the earlier, less powerful stock versions such as the 1964½ Ford Mustang that had a six-cylinder engine. Next came the 289 cc V-8 engine. The public's clamor for ever more powerful engines was answered by the industry's introduction of the 390 cc engine. This ended in the Shelby Mustang GT variant with the awesome Cleveland Boss engine. Not to be outdone, General Motors introduced its Oldsmobile 442, Chevelle SS 396, and Camaro. Chrysler's Fury and Road Runner soon joined the pack. These cars, often featured in Hollywood film chase scenes such as that made famous by Steve McQueen in <u>Bullit</u>, were targeted at a youth market, late teenagers and young adults who often used the cars as a status symbol. Muscle cars could be seen lining the pits of drag races on Saturday nights and cruising the city's main streets and hamburger drive-ins on the weekend. Youths could be seen driving around mall parking lots in their thundering, glass-pack exhausted behemoths, trying to impress the opposite sex. The popularity of the muscle car was brought down by the oil embargo of the 1970s, which brought long lines at gasoline stations, fuel rationing, and increasing prices. The love affair with these cars, though, continues, if only as a form of nostalgia.

ANSWERS TO EXERCISE 22: REVISING SENTENCE FRAGMENTS

Most college athletes are caught in a conflict between their athletic and academic careers. Sometimes college athletes' responsibilities on the playing field make it hard for them to be good students. Often athletes must make a choice between sports and a degree. Some athletes would not be able to afford college without athletic scholarships. But, ironically, their commitments to sports (training, exercise, practice, and travel to out-of-town games, for example) deprive athletes of valuable classroom time. The role of college athletes is constantly being questioned. Critics suggest they exist only to participate in and promote college athletics. Because of the importance of this role to academic institutions, scandals occasionally develop, with coaches and even faculty members arranging to inflate athletes' grades to help them remain eligible for participation in sports. Some universities even lower admissions standards. To help remedy this and other inequities, the controversial Proposition 48, passed at the NCAA convention in 1982, established minimum scores on aptitude tests. But many people feel the NCAA remains overly concerned with profits rather than education. As a result, college athletic competition is increasingly coming to resemble pro sports, from the coaches' pressure on the players to win to the network television exposure to the wagers on the games' outcomes.

ANSWERS TO EXERCISE 23: REVISING SENTENCE FRAGMENTS

The Stock Market crashed in 1929. The speculative boom in stocks that seemed unending came to a screeching halt in October on the day that has come to be known as Black Monday. This day caused an entire generation to distrust investing in equities. At first, the far-reaching effects of the crash were not understood. They seemed to affect directly only those who owned stocks and bonds. These people lost their entire fortune in one afternoon. Some financially devastated individuals saw no alternative other than suicide, leaping from the windows of tall buildings on Wall Street. Soon, though, the awful truth became apparent. The entire country slowly slid into economic despair known as the Great Depression which lasted for an entire decade. Companies went out of business, jobs were scarce, food lines began to form. Men left their families to ride the rails as hobos, looking for any job they could find. The desperation seemed unending until the federal government intervened by creating the WPA, a program designed to build public works projects such as dams and roadways, to employ large numbers of people. The economic depression was not ended, though, until the country entered World War II. when military production energized the flagging economy. True to the inherent nature of market cycles, the revived economy created the market's next upward move. It was spurred by the Baby Boomers' pouring money into the market to provide for their own retirement. But the lessons learned from the Crash of '29 and the cyclical nature of the market have to be relearned by each succeeding generation. Will the current mania and rampant speculation lead to tomorrow's Black Tuesday or Black Wednesday when the retiring Boomers are forced to withdraw their funds from the stock market to finance their lifestyles?

ANSWERS TO EXERCISE 24: REVISING SENTENCE FRAGMENTS

The domestic responsibilities of Colonial women were many, their fates sealed by the absence of mechanical devices that have eased the burdens of women in recent years. Washing clothes, for instance, was a complicated procedure, the primary problem being the moving of some 50 gallons of water from a pump or well to the stove (for heating) and washtub (for soaking and scrubbing). Home cooking also presented difficulties, the main challenges for the housewife being the danger of inadvertently poisoning her family and the rarity of ovens. Even much later, housework was extremely time-consuming, especially for rural and low-income families, their access to labor-saving devices remaining relatively limited. (Just before World War II, for instance, only 35 percent of farm residences in the United States had electricity.)

ANSWERS TO EXERCISE 25: REVISING SENTENCE FRAGMENTS

Malls dominate the shopping and the popular cultural center of many cities, offering a myriad of stores and entertainment for people of all ages. Most malls are centered around an anchor store, an outlet of a large national chain, such as Sears or Penney's or Marshalls. In addition, many smaller, specialty stores are housed in the mall, for example Nordic Trak, Walden Books, kitchen shops, and computer stores. These stores feature a variety of merchandise targeted to specific hobbies or interests: the exercise enthusiast, the voracious reader, the gourmand, and the technophile. After hours of shopping, customers are ready to eat. Malls anticipate this need by providing a plethora of food establishments from food courts to sit-down restaurants. Hamburgers, to pizzas, to Chinese food, to buffets, to haute cuisine are available. Entertainment is offered too, such as carousel rides for children to video arcades for teenagers to the multi-screened theaters for all ages. Other than shopping, eating, and playing, many people find the malls convenient gathering places to meet friends, to exercise, or just to escape inclement weather. For example, large groups of teens gather in the main concourse. Older people walk laps around the concourse. The mall has become almost like a home away from home for many people.

ANSWERS TO EXERCISE 26: REVISING SENTENCE FRAGMENTS

One of the phenomena of the 1990s is the number of parents determined to raise "superbabies." Many affluent parents, professionals themselves, seem driven to raise children who are mentally superior and physically fit as well. To this end, they enroll babies as young as a few weeks old in baby gyms and sign up slightly older preschool children for classes that teach computer skills or violin or swimming or Japanese. Such classes are important, but are not the only source of formal education for very young children. Parents themselves try to raise their babies' IQs or learn to teach toddlers to read or to do simple math. Some parents begin teaching with flash cards when their babies are only a few months—or days—old. Others wait until their children are a bit older and enroll them in day-care programs designed to sharpen their skills or spend thousands of dollars on "educational toys." Some psychologists and child-care professionals are favorably impressed by this trend toward earlier and earlier education. But most have serious reservations, feeling the emphasis on academics and pressure to achieve may stunt children's social and emotional growth.

ANSWERS TO EXERCISE 27: REVISING SENTENCE FRAGMENTS

The pursuit of the aquatic species, otherwise known as the sport of fishing, encompasses a variety of choices depending on one's locale. Coastal residents are afforded the opportunity to fish for a multitude of salt-water species, including shallow water dwellers such as bone fish, snook, and tarpon. Deep water inhabitants include varieties such as red snapper, amberjack, and tuna. Although inland fishermen may not have the number of species to choose from, they have a much larger variety of watery locales such as rivers, lakes, creeks, and ponds which harbor the common species of bass, bream, and catfish among others. Techniques and tackle used depend on the locale. From the large spooled and heavy-lined salt-water reel to the bait-casting reel to the cane pole, these reels can be installed on a large range of rods and line combinations, such as bamboo to fiberglass to exotic composites of space-age materials. In addition, the fisherman is faced with the choice of several types of bait from artificial lures to live bait fish to the lowly worm. Regardless of where one chooses to fish or what type of rig is used, fishing provides two benefits: fare for the table and a great source of relaxation and pleasure. As an old sage once said, "Since the earth is two-thirds water, man should spend two-thirds of his time fishing."

ANSWERS TO EXERCISE 28: REVISING COMMA SPLICES AND FUSED SENTENCES

Answers will vary. To illustrate the various responses, each sentence below is followed with the four possible types of corrections. Class discussion should consider the need to balance the types of choices in a piece of writing rather than adhering to a single method of correction.

Writing with a word processor has made editing papers much easier, many corrections can be done with a simple keystroke.

1. easier. Many
2. easier; many
3. easier, for
4. Writing with a word processor has made editing papers much easier, many corrections done with a simple keystroke.

No longer is it necessary to correct non-standard punctuation by hand running the risk of introducing new errors during the editing stage is now virtually eliminated.

1. hand. Running
2. hand; running
3. hand, for
4. No longer is it necessary to correct non-standard punctuation by hand, virtually eliminating the risk of introducing new errors during the editing stage.

The essay, which has been saved on disk or in hard memory, can simply be restored to the screen for viewing the corrections can then be inserted into the text and re-saved.

1. viewing. The
2. viewing; the
3. viewing, and the
4. The essay, which has been saved on disk or in hard memory, can simply be restored to the screen for viewing, with corrections inserted into the text and re-saved.

The ease of this process has made writers more likely to proofread their work with care, this results in a better quality of work as well as improved grades.

1. care. This
2. care; this
3. care, and this
4. The ease of this process has made writers more likely to proofread their work with care, resulting in a better quality of work as well as improved grades.

For most students the days of laboriously handwriting or typing multiple drafts of essays are gone, the computer has closed that chapter of the writing process.

1. gone. The
2. gone; the
3. gone, for the
4. For most students the days of laboriously handwriting or typing multiple drafts of essays are gone, the computer having closed that chapter of the writing process.

ANSWERS TO EXERCISE 29: SENTENCE COMBINING

Answers will vary.

1. Several recent studies indicate that many American high school students have a poor sense of history; this is affecting our future as a democratic nation and as individuals.
2. Surveys show that nearly one-third of American 17-year-olds cannot identify the countries the United States fought against in World War II, and one-third think Columbus reached the New World after 1750.

3. Several reasons have been given for this decline in historical literacy, but the main reason is the way history is taught.
4. Although this problem is bad news, the good news is that there is increasing agreement among educators about what is wrong with current methods of teaching history.
5. History can be exciting and engaging, but too often it is presented in a boring manner.
6. Students are typically expected to memorize dates, facts, and figures; history as adventure—as a "good story"—is frequently neglected.
7. One way to avoid this problem is to use good textbooks, which should be accurate, lively, and focused.
8. Another way to create student interest in historical events is to use primary sources instead of so-called "comprehensive" textbooks, for autobiographies, journals, and diaries can give students insight into larger issues.
9. Students can also be challenged to think about history by taking sides in a debate, and they can learn more about connections between historical events by writing essays rather than taking multiple-choice tests.
10. Finally, history teachers should be less concerned about specific historical details, and they should be more concerned about conveying the wonder of history.

ANSWERS TO EXERCISE 30: SUBJECT-VERB AGREEMENT

1. Subject and verb agree in spite of intervening words.
2. Compound subject preceded by *every* takes singular verb.
3. Singular subject takes singular verb despite plural form.
4. Collective noun referring to the group as a unit takes a singular verb.
5. Verb agrees with the singular antecedent of the relative pronoun.
6. Singular indefinite pronoun takes singular verb.
7. Linking verb agrees with subject, not with subject complement.
8. Linking verb agrees with subject, not with subject complement.
9. Singular subject in plural form takes singular verb.
10. Subject and verb agree in inverted word order.

Answers to Exercise 31:
Subject-Verb Agreement

1. correct
2. correct
3. Both the subject and the verb <u>have</u> to agree in number for the sentence to be correct.
4. If otters, fish, and insects <u>swim</u> in the same pond, some will be eaten by the others.
5. Neither country music nor rap <u>appeals</u> to me.
6. The tree filled with birdhouses <u>attracts</u> many different species of birds.
7. correct
8. No matter how many people enter the contest, only one of the contestants <u>is</u> going to win the prize.
9. correct
10. correct

Answers to Exercise 32: Subject-Verb, Pronoun-Antecedent Agreement

1. correct
2. Vinyl records, which came in three different sizes, 78, 45, and 33 revolutions per minute, <u>have</u> been replaced in popularity by the compact discs.
3. Although some bargains are available, a collector can invest a large sum on <u>his</u> or <u>her</u> music library.
4. correct
5. Unlike records and tapes which can lose <u>their</u> sound quality because of needle scratches or shredding, discs theoretically <u>last</u> forever.
6. Compact discs use a new digital technology which <u>was</u> unavailable when records were popular.
7. Every audiophile <u>delights</u> in showing off <u>his</u> or <u>her</u> music collection and equipment.
8. correct
9. In spite of <u>their</u> advantages, the one drawback to compact discs is the inability to record music.
10. The nostalgia many feel for the vinyl records will someday be felt for discs when <u>they</u> <u>are</u> replaced by the silicon chip.

Answers to Exercise 33: Subject-Verb, Pronoun-Antecedent Agreement

You might refer students to the section on sexist language in conjunction with this exercise.

1. The governess and the cook are seemingly pursued by evil as they try to protect Miles and Flora from those seeking to possess the children's souls.
2. The insulin-dependent diabetic is now able to take advantage of new technology that can help alleviate his or her symptoms.
3. Every homeowner in shore regions worries about the possible effects of a hurricane on his or her property.
4. Federally funded job-training programs offer the unskilled worker an opportunity to acquire skills he or she can use to secure employment.
5. The foreign import poses a major challenge to the American automobile market.
6. *Brideshead Revisited* tells how one family affects Charles Ryder.
7. *Writer's Digest* and *The Writer* are designed to aid the writer as he or she seeks markets for his or her work.
8. Almost every American family has access to television; in fact, more have televisions than have indoor plumbing.
9. In Montana, it seems as though all the towns' elevations are higher than their populations.
10. Women without men are like fish without bicycles.

Answers to Exercise 34: Principal Parts

Eric Blair, a well-known British novelist and essayist, *chose* to use the pseudonym George Orwell. His essay "A Hanging," *taken* from his book *Shooting an Elephant and Other Essays*, is *written* in narrative form. It describes a morning in Burma when Orwell observed the execution of a prisoner who was to be *hanged* for his crime. One of the most startling scenes in the essay comes at the end when onlookers, *forsaking* the seriousness of the moment, leave the prison yard after the event, laughing on their way to have a drink.

Answers to Exercise 35: Principal Parts

1. sat
2. well
3. hanged

4. Lying
5. well, good

ANSWERS TO EXERCISE 36: TENSE

1. settled, engaged
2. have been
3. resulting
4. had continued
5. broke
6. have been operating
7. are following
8. had begun
9. zone
10. will be enjoying

ANSWERS TO EXERCISE 37: TENSE

1. declares
2. has learned
3. was
4. have given
5. became (happened before the action of the play)
6. married (happened before the action of the play)
7. accuses
8. learns

ANSWERS TO EXERCISE 38: MOOD

performed
challenged
were
was
give
nail
place
stepped
see

ANSWERS TO EXERCISE 39: VOICE

1. stock market <u>began</u> - active
2. landmark <u>was accepted</u> - passive

Answers to Numbered Exercises

3. contracts <u>were required</u> - passive
4. contracts <u>represented</u> - active
   traders <u>referred</u> - active
5. traders <u>moved</u> - active
6. advent <u>allowed</u> - active

ANSWERS TO EXERCISE 40: VOICE

The Chinese invented rockets about 1000 A.D. They packed gunpowder into bamboo tubes and ignited it by means of a fuse. Soldiers fired these rockets at enemy armies and usually caused panic. In thirteenth-century England Roger Bacon introduced an improved form of gunpowder. As a result, soldiers used rockets as a common—although unreliable—weapon in battle. In the early eighteenth century William Congreve, an English artillery expert, constructed a twenty-pound rocket that traveled almost two miles. By the late nineteenth century the physicist Ernst Mach gave thought to supersonic speeds. He predicted the sonic boom. In America, Robert Goddard launched the first liquid fuel rocket in 1926. He wrote a pamphlet that anticipated almost all future rocket developments. As a result of his pioneering work, he is called the father of modern rocketry.

ANSWERS TO EXERCISE 41: VOICE

Answers will vary.

The Regent Diamond is one of the world's most famous and coveted jewels. The 410-carat diamond was discovered by a slave in 1701 in an Indian mine. (Emphasis is on the diamond rather than on who discovered it.) Over the years, it was stolen and sold several times. (Emphasis is on what happened rather than on *people*.) In 1717, the Regent of France bought the diamond for an enormous sum, but during the French Revolution, it disappeared again. It was later discovered in a ditch in Paris. (Emphasis is on its eventual discovery rather than on who discovered it.) Eventually, Napoleon had the diamond set into his ceremonial sword. At last, when the French monarch fell, the Regent Diamond was placed in the Louvre where it still remains to be enjoyed by all. (Emphasis is on where it was placed rather than on who placed it there.)

ANSWERS TO EXERCISE 42: PRONOUN CASE

1. he
2. him
3. she
4. me
5. us
6. who
7. We
8. your
9. me

ANSWERS TO EXERCISE 43: SENTENCE COMBINING

1. Toni Morrison is an award-winning American writer whose subject matter often focuses on African-American themes.
2. Robin Cook, another popular writer, whose subjects exclusively deal with common people caught up in exotic medical dilemmas, holds a medical degree.
3. Steve Nison who wrote *Japanese Candlestick Charting Techniques* in 1990, also wrote a companion book, *Beyond Candlesticks*, in 1994.
4. Erle Stanley Gardner who wrote numerous detective mysteries, created the famous character Perry Mason, the well-known attorney who lost only one case in his entire career.
5. Ayn Rand, whose *Atlas Shrugged* and *The Fountainhead* remain perennial best sellers, is the icon of generations of college-aged students.

ANSWERS TO EXERCISE 44: PRONOUN REFERENCE

1. remote antecedent
   "It" refers to <u>evaluation</u> mentioned in the preceding sentence. Repeat the noun to make the meaning clearer.
2. nonexistent antecedent
   "They" has no stated antecedent. Supply an appropriate plural noun to eliminate this problem.
3. ambiguous antecedent
   The referent for "it" is unclear; it could refer to <u>committee</u>, <u>form</u>, or <u>process</u>. Including the appropriate noun will remove the ambiguity.

4. ambiguous antecedent or nonexistent antecedent
   It is unclear whether he, she, they refers to the supervisor or to another person named to complete the evaluation. Supplying the name of the person expected to be successful would eliminate the confusion.
5. remote antecedent
   "This" refers to complaints in the previous sentence. Repeat the word to eliminate the error.
6. ambiguous antecedent
   "Their" could refer to either staff or customers. Repeat the noun to eliminate the error.
7. nonexistent antecedent
   "They" has no referent in the sentence. Include noun the pronoun clearly refers to.
8. nonexistent antecedent
   "She" has no referent in the sentence. Include noun the pronoun clearly refers to.
9. ambiguous antecedent
   "She" could refer to either "Margaret" or to the "other woman." Repeat the appropriate noun to make the reference clear.
10. remote antecedent
    "It" refers to "suggestion box" in the previous sentence. Replace the pronoun with the noun to eliminate the confusion.

ANSWERS TO EXERCISE 45: MODIFICATION

The most popular self-help trend in the United States today is subliminal tapes. These tapes, with titles like "How to Attract Love," "Freedom from Acne," and "I Am a Genius," are intended to solve every problem known to modern society—quickly and easily. The tapes are said to work because their "hidden messages" bypass conscious defense mechanisms. The listener hears only music or relaxing sounds, like waves rolling slowly and steadily. At decibel levels perceived only subconsciously, positive words and phrases are embedded, usually by someone who speaks deeply and rhythmically. The top-selling cassettes are those to help you lose weight or quit smoking. The popularity of such tapes is not difficult to understand. They promise easy solutions to complex problems. But the main benefit of these tapes appears to be for the sellers, who are accumulating profits really quickly.

ANSWERS TO EXERCISE 46: SENTENCE MODELING

Answers will vary.

1. David seemed tired.
   Jerry was anxious.
   Lienne appeared happy.
   Maggie is depressed.
   Chris remained confident.

2. Julie finds her job interesting.
   I thought his speech dull.
   The reviewers deemed the play fascinating.
   The students found the course helpful.
   Charles proved the problem unsolvable.

ANSWERS TO EXERCISE 47: COMPARATIVE AND SUPERLATIVE FORMS

1. many/more/most
2. eccentric/more eccentric/most eccentric
3. confusing/more confusing/most confusing
4. bad/worse/worst
5. mysterious/more mysterious/most mysterious
6. softly/more softly/most softly
7. embarrassing/more embarrassing/most embarrassing
8. well/better/best
9. often/more often/most often
10. tiny/tinier/tiniest
11. easy/easier/easiest
12. judicious/more judicious/most judicious

Sentences will vary.

ANSWERS TO EXERCISE 48: NOUNS AS MODIFIERS

Part I: Nouns used as adjectives are underlined.

The <u>student government business management trainee</u> program is extremely popular on campus. The <u>student</u> government donated some of the <u>seed</u> money to begin this <u>management trainee</u> program, which is one of the most successful the <u>university business</u> school has ever offered to <u>undergraduate</u> students. Three <u>core</u> courses must be taken

Answers to Numbered Exercises 19

before the <u>student</u> intern can actually begin work. First, a <u>management theory</u> course is given every <u>spring</u> semester in conjunction with the <u>business</u> school. Then, the following <u>fall</u> semester, students in the <u>trainee</u> program are required to take a course in <u>personnel</u> practices, including <u>employee</u> benefits. Finally, they take a <u>business</u> elective.

During the summer, the <u>student</u> interns are placed in <u>junior management</u> positions in large <u>electronics, manufacturing,</u> or <u>public utility</u> companies. This <u>job</u> experience is considered the most valuable part of the program because it gives students a taste of the <u>work</u> world.

Part II (revised paragraph): Answers will vary.

ANSWERS TO EXERCISE 49: COMBINING FOR VARIETY

First published in 1611, the Authorized Version of the Bible (often referred to as the King James Version) involved several years of work by numerous scholars. Much of the year prior to its publication was devoted to final preparations before sending the document to press. One of the many steps taken during those final months involved calling upon several of the eminent writers of the day to "refine" this most recent of English translations. These writers devoted their efforts to enhancing the poetic qualities of such books as Proverbs, the Song of Solomon, and the Psalms. We should not be surprised to learn that William Shakespeare was among this group of writers. Although he had not yet secured the reputation that he is universally granted today, he had achieved a great deal of success and popularity as a playwright and poet.

ANSWERS TO EXERCISE 50: COMBINING FOR VARIETY

1. a. One of the more intriguing literary legends surrounding the King James Version of the Bible alleges that Shakespeare's hand is present in the 46th Psalm.
   b. Turn to the psalm to see for yourself.
2. a. By counting to the forty-sixth word from the beginning of the psalm (*shake*) and then by identifying the forty-sixth word form the end of the psalm (*spear*), we find what might he dismissed as merely interesting coincidence.
   b. These findings might be dismissed as merely interesting coincidence.
3. a. The situation becomes all the more intriguing when we realize that Shakespeare was forty-six years old when the revision work was underway in 1610.

b. We shouldn't be surprised to find that Shakespeare played a role in translating this magnificently poetic portion of the King James Version.
c. One of the more intriguing literary legends surrounding the King James Version of the Bible alleges that Shakespeare's hand is present in the 46th Psalm. Turn to the psalm to see for yourself. Count to the forty-sixth word from the beginning of the psalm (*shake*) and then identify the forty-sixth word form the end of the psalm (*spear*). These findings might be dismissed as merely interesting coincidence. The situation becomes all the more intriguing, however, when we realize that Shakespeare was forty-six years old when the revision work was underway in 1610. We shouldn't be surprised to find that Shakespeare played a role in translating this magnificently poetic portion of the King James Version.

ANSWERS TO EXERCISE 51: REVISING FOR VARIETY

Among the most easily recognized works of art, Leonardo da Vinci's *The Last Supper* was produced during the artist's residence in Milan and under the patronage of Duke Sforza. Using oil and tempera, Leonardo chose as his "canvas" a wall in the refectory of Santa Maria della Grazie. While even the most casual art observer has viewed a copy of *The Last Supper,* few serious students of art realize that it is actually a mural, measuring 14'–5" × 28'. That Leonardo completed his work on such a large scale is somewhat surprising to many who have seen only small replicas—many of them the size of a post card.

Giorgio Vasari, the Italian art historian who lived during the sixteenth century, records an interesting anecdote concerning Leonardo's use of models for *The Last Supper*. For his models of the disciples, Leonardo drew from life, encountering difficulty only in locating a suitable Judas Iscariot. Throughout much of his work on the painting, Leonardo was troubled by the prior of Santa Maria, who monitored the work's progress from a vantage uncomfortably close for the artist. Upon hearing that the prior had expressed his concerns to Duke Sforza, Leonardo mentioned that any delay he had experienced was merely the result of his having encountered difficulty in identifying a model for the betrayer. But, Leonardo pointed out, he would be delayed no longer, for he had located his model: the prior would serve nicely.

ANSWERS TO EXERCISE 52: REVISING FOR VARIETY

What a day of excitement! When the Fourth of July comes around, the nation explodes with patriotism. Everywhere we look, we see parades and picnics, firecrackers and fireworks. An outsider might wonder what all the fuss is about. *What could we tell this person?* We could explain that this is America's birthday party, and all the candles are being lit at once. There is no reason for us to hold back our enthusiasm—or to limit the noise that celebrates it. *So join in.* The Fourth of July is watermelon and corn on the cob, American flags and sparklers, brass bands and more. Everyone looks forward to this celebration, and everyone has a good time.

ANSWERS TO EXERCISE 53: OPENING STRATEGIES

Answers will vary.

1. When he was a very young child, Momaday was taken to Devil's Tower, the geological formation in Wyoming that is called Tsoai (Bear Tree) in Kiowa, and given the name Tsoai-talee (Bear Tree Boy). (adverb clause)
2. In the Kiowa myth of the origin of Tsoai, a boy playfully chases his seven sisters up a tree, which rises into the air as the boy is transformed into a bear. (prepositional phrase)
3. Becoming increasingly ferocious, the bear-boy claws the bark of the tree, which becomes a great rock with a flat top and deeply scored sides. (participial phrase)
4. Eventually, after climbing higher and higher to escape their brother's wrath, the sisters become the seven stars of the Big Dipper. (adverb)
5. A constant in Momaday's works, this story from which he received one of his names appears in *The Way to Rainy Mountain, House Made of Dawn,* and *The Ancient Child.* (appositive)

ANSWERS TO EXERCISE 54: REVISING FOR VARIETY

1. A band called the Beach Boys—consisting of Brian Wilson, his brothers Carl and Dennis, their cousin Mike Love, and Alan Jardine, a friend—was formed in 1961.
2. Attracting national attention was the group's first single, "Surfin'."
3. Capitol Records, feeling the band had potential, signed the group to record "Surfin' Safari."

4. Writing, arranging, and producing most of the other top-twenty singles during the next five years was Brian Wilson.
5. Their songs, focusing on California sun and good times, included "I Get Around," "Be True to Your School," "Fun, Fun, Fun," and "Good Vibrations."

ANSWERS TO EXERCISE 55: REVISING FOR EMPHASIS

1. Because criminals are better armed than ever before, police want to upgrade their firepower.
2. A few years ago felons used small-caliber six-shot revolvers—so-called Saturday night specials.
3. Now these weapons have been replaced by semiautomatic pistols capable of firing fifteen to twenty rounds, along with paramilitary weapons like the AK-47.
4. In order to gain equal footing with their adversaries, police are adopting new fast-firing shotguns and 9mm automatic pistols.
5. Automatic pistols, the weapon of choice among law enforcement officers, have numerous advantages over the traditional .38-caliber police revolver, including faster reloading and a hair trigger.

ANSWERS TO EXERCISE 56: REVISING FOR EMPHASIS

Answers will vary; a possible version appears below.

For thousands of years, the Nile Valley experienced an annual flood. The Nile's floodwaters carried soil particles from upstream, deposited them throughout the flood plain, and renewed the fertility of the Egyptian fields. Although it might be interpreted as a natural disaster, the yearly event permitted the rise of one of the richest and most advanced ancient civilizations. The flood enabled people to grow enough food to support a large population, allowing time for other activities, including building, scholarship, and art.

During the past century, construction of the Aswan High Dam has brought enormous changes to the Nile Valley. The dam is designed to retain an entire annual flow of the Nile and provide power to make cheap fertilizers, which are needed by the intensively cultivated farms that are no longer covered by silty Nile water. The dam has ended the Nile Valley's annual flood, which used to bring the region nutritious silt that was once cherished for its nutrients. Many people now consider the silt a nuisance because it fills up irrigation canals.

ANSWERS TO EXERCISE 57: ACTIVE VOICE FOR EMPHASIS

Jack Dempsey, the heavyweight champion between 1919 and 1926, had an interesting but uneven career. Many considered him one of the greatest boxers of all time. Dempsey began fighting as "Kid Blackie," but his career didn't take off until 1919, when Jack "Doc" Kearns became his manager. Dempsey won the championship when he defeated Jess Willard in Toledo, Ohio, in 1919. Dempsey immediately became a popular sports figure; Franklin Delano Roosevelt was one of his biggest fans. Jack Dempsey made influential friends; gave boxing lessons to the actor Rudolph Valentino; made friends with Douglas Fairbanks, Sr., Damon Runyon, and J. Paul Getty; and made Hollywood serials. But he lost the title to Gene Tunney and failed to regain it in the following year. Meanwhile, unpleasant developments such as a bitter legal battle with his manager and his 1920 indictment for draft evasion marred his life. In subsequent years, after his boxing career declined, Dempsey opened a restaurant and attended many major sporting events. This exposure kept him in the public eye until he lost his restaurant. Jack Dempsey died in 1983.

ANSWERS TO EXERCISE 58: REVISING FOR CONCISENESS

Sally Ride, an astrophysicist, was the first American woman astronaut. NASA selected Ride as an astronaut in 1978 because she was a first-rate athlete and had done graduate work in X-ray astronomy and free-electron lasers. Earlier, while she was a graduate student at Stanford, Ride knew she could become a theoretical physicist. At NASA she helped to design the space shuttle's remote manipulator arm, and later she relayed flight instructions to astronauts until she was assigned to a flight crew. Now, Ride teaches at the University of California. Although Ride is no longer a NASA employee, she remains something special: America's first woman in space.

ANSWERS TO EXERCISE 59: REVISING FOR CONCISENESS

The seven daughters of Atlas, known as the Pleiades, were pursued by Orion, who was unable to seize any of them. Orion continued to follow them until Zeus took pity on them and placed them in the heavens. Although seven stars make up the Pleiades, only six stars are clearly visible. The seventh is invisible except to those who have especially keen vision. In Greek mythology, the seventh star represented Electra, mother of Dardanus, who founded the Trojan race. The legend held that, rather than look down upon the destruction of Troy, Electra dropped from the sky. Today, though, with the aid of binoculars, well over seven stars are visible in this cluster. Viewing through a telescope yields several hundred.

ANSWERS TO EXERCISE 60: REVISING FOR CONCISENESS

Having lost the trail of the Pleiades, Orion became the companion of the virgin huntress Artemis—goddess of the moon and twin sister of Apollo. Fearing for his sister's chastity, Apollo sent a large scorpion to chase Orion. When Orion observed the scorpion enter a body of water, he pursued the beast. Apollo then persuaded Artemis to shoot the object that bobbed in the waves, and her arrow pierced Orion's head. Deeply saddened at her loss, Artemis placed Orion's image among the stars, where it continues to be stalked by the constellation of the scorpion, although the two are separated by a great distance. In front of Orion, however, and much closer to him are the Pleiades, whom he continues to pursue.

ANSWERS TO EXERCISE 61: SHIFTS IN TENSE, VOICE, MOOD, PERSON, NUMBER

1. Gettysburg is a borough of south-central Pennsylvania where some of the bloodiest fighting of the Civil War occurred in July of 1863.
2. correct
3. The early Babylonians divided the circle into 360 parts and could calculate the volume of a pyramid.
4. During World War II General Motors expanded its production facilities and made guns, tanks, and ammunition.
5. correct
6. First clear the area of weeds, and then spread the mulch in a six-inch layer.
7. When one visits the Grand Canyon, one should be sure to notice the fractures and faults on the north side of the Kaibab Plateau.
8. For a wine grape, cool weather means it will have a higher acid content and a sour taste; hot weather means it will have a lower acid content and a sweet taste.
9. correct
10. When you look at the Angora goat, you will see it has an abundant undergrowth.
11. Robert the Bruce defeated the English forces at Bannockburn, and soon thereafter he was recognized as King of Scotland.

12. During the mummification process, the Egyptians placed many of the body's organs in canopic jars; ironically, though, they discarded the brain because they were uncertain of its role.
13. Scholars have often sought to determine the actual location of Gulliver's Brobdingnag, but they have been unable to pinpoint it on the map.
14. In spite of a disappointing record of three wins and eleven losses, Coach DeGaetano was proud that the team had maintained a positive attitude and that it received the League Sportsmanship Trophy.

Answers to Exercise 62: Shifts from Direct to Indirect Discourse

1. In cases of possible sexual harassment, Ellen Goodman suggests a "reasonable woman standard" be applied. We should ask how a reasonable woman would interpret the situation and how a reasonable woman would behave.
2. Sally Thane Christensen, advocating the use of an endangered species of tree, the yew, as a treatment for cancer, asked whether a tree was worth a life.
3. Stephen Nathanson, considering the morality of the death penalty, asked what we would think if the death penalty actually saved lives.
4. Martin Luther King, Jr., said that he had a dream that one day this nation would rise up and live out the true meaning of its creed.
5. Mohandas K. Gandhi wrote that complete civil disobedience is a state of peaceful rebellion—a refusal to obey every single State-made law.
6. Benjamin Franklin once stated that the older he grew, the more apt he was to doubt his own judgment of others.
7. Speaking of the theater of the absurd in 1962, Edward Albee asked if it was, as it had been accused of being, obscure, sordid, destructive, anti-theater, perverse, and absurd (in the sense of foolish).
8. Thoreau said that the finest qualities of our nature, like the bloom on fruits, can be preserved only by the most delicate handling.
9. In *Death Knocks*, Death asks Nat whom he should look like.
10. In *Death of a Salesman*, Linda stands by her husband's grave after his funeral and asks why no one came.
11. In F. Scott Fitzgerald's *The Great Gatsby*, Jay Gatsby observes that Daisy's voice is full of money.

12. About the importance of fostering family values, Vice President Dan Quayle stated in a 1992 speech that it's time to talk again about family, hard work, integrity and personal responsibility.

ANSWERS TO EXERCISE 63: MIXED CONSTRUCTIONS

Answers will vary.

1. Implementing the "motor voter" bill will make it easier for people to register to vote.
2. They won the game because she sank the basket.
3. Because of a defect in design, the roof of the Hartford Stadium collapsed.
4. Since he wants to make his paper clearer, he revises extensively.
5. Even though she works for a tobacco company, she should not necessarily be against prohibiting smoking in restaurants.

ANSWERS TO EXERCISE 64: FAULTY PREDICATION

Answers will vary.

1. Inflation is a decline in the purchasing power of currency.
2. Hypertension is elevated blood pressure.
3. Machines containing computers, such as instant cash machines, have become part of our everyday lives.
4. Some people say that increasing violence in American cities results from guns being too easily available.
5. American cities are congested because too many people live too close together.

ANSWERS TO EXERCISE 65: INCOMPLETE OR ILLOGICAL COMPARISONS

1. Opportunities in technical writing are more promising than those in business writing. (illogical comparison)
2. Technical writing is more challenging than business writing. (incomplete comparison)
3. In some ways, technical and business writing require more attention to correctness than other forms of writing and are, therefore, more difficult. (incomplete comparison)
4. Business writers are concerned about clarity as much as technical writers are. (illogical comparison)

5. Technology-based industries may one day create more writing opportunities than any other industry. (illogical comparison)

ANSWERS TO EXERCISE 66: USING PARALLELISM

1. Angela [worked all of her math problems], [studied her Spanish assignment], [read two history textbook chapters], and then [wrote her composition].
2. Long before she began to write professionally, Lindsay had developed a habit of [observing people], [storing impressions they made upon her], and [drawing conclusions about human beings from them].
3. Before making the long journey to Panama City Beach for spring break, take these precautions: [change the oil], [fill the gas tank], [check the tires' air pressure], and [replace the windshield wipers].
4. Brian and Beth agreed that it was one of the best films they'd seen in several months: [its characters were believable], [its camera work was intriguing], [its soundtrack was spectacular], and [its language was not offensive].
5. For a fishing trip that's certain to be memorable, my grandfather recommends the following preparations: [pack your rod, reel, and tackle box]; [check the boat's motor]; [purchase gas and oil]; and [make plenty of peanut butter and jelly sandwiches].

ANSWERS TO EXERCISE 67: SENTENCE COMBINING

1. Originally there were five performing Marx Brothers: Groucho, Chico, Harpo, Gummo, and Zeppo.
2. Groucho, Chico, and Harpo were very well known, but first Gummo and later Zeppo dropped out of the act.
3. They began in vaudeville before World War I and opened their first show, "I'll Say She Is," in New York in 1924.
4. The Marx Brothers' first movie, *The Coconuts*, was followed by *Animal Crackers, Monkey Business, Horsefeathers, Duck Soup,* and *A Night at the Opera*.
5. In each of these movies, the Marx Brothers make people laugh and establish a unique, zany comic style.
6. In their movies, each man has a set of familiar trademarks: Groucho has a mustache and a long coat, wiggles his eyebrows, and smokes a cigar; Chico always wears a funny hat and affects a phony Italian accent; Harpo never speaks.

7. Groucho is always cast as a sly operator who tries to cheat people out of their money and to charm women.
8. In *The Coconuts* he plays Mr. Hammer, proprietor of the run-down Coconut Manor, a Florida hotel; in *Horsefeathers* he plays Professor Quincy Adams Wagstaff, president of Huxley College, which also has financial problems.
9. In *Duck Soup* Groucho plays Rufus T. Firefly, president of the country of Fredonia, which was formerly ruled by the late husband of a Mrs. Teasdale and is now at war with the country of Sylvania.
10. Margaret Dumont, often Groucho's "leading lady," plays Mrs. Teasdale in *Duck Soup,* Mrs. Claypool in *A Night at the Opera,* and Mrs. Potter in *The Coconuts.*

ANSWERS TO EXERCISE 68: CORRECTING FAULTY PARALLELISM

1. The world is divided between <u>those who wear galoshes</u> and <u>those who discover continents</u>.
2. <u>Soviet leaders, members of Congress,</u> and <u>American Catholic bishops</u> all pressed the president to limit the arms race. (C)
3. A national task force on education recommended improving public education <u>by making the school day longer,</u> <u>by raising teachers' salaries</u> and <u>by integrating more technology into the curriculum.</u>
4. The fast-food industry is expanding to include many kinds of restaurants: <u>those that serve pizza,</u> <u>those that serve fried chicken,</u> <u>those that serve Mexican-style food</u> and <u>those that serve hamburgers.</u>
5. Many Scotch drinkers in the United States are switching to wine or beer because of <u>high prices,</u> <u>changing tastes,</u> and <u>increased health awareness.</u>
6. With summer just around the corner, I'm looking forward to <u>swimming in our pool,</u> <u>fishing at the lake,</u> and <u>grilling in our back yard.</u>
7. Brian has developed a challenging training program: <u>before breakfast, he jogs;</u> <u>after lunch, he bikes;</u> and <u>after supper, he swims.</u>

ANSWERS TO EXERCISE 69: IDENTIFYING HEADWORDS

1. He wore his <u>almost</u> new jeans. [He wore his nearly new jeans.]

   He <u>almost</u> wore his new jeans. [He decided at the last minute not to wear his new jeans.]

2. He <u>only</u> had three dollars in his pocket. [Besides the three dollars, he had nothing else in his pocket.]

   <u>Only</u> he had three dollars in his pocket. [He alone had this amount of money in his pocket.]

3. I don't <u>even</u> like freshwater fish. [I really dislike them.]

   I don't like <u>even</u> freshwater fish. [I dislike all kinds of fish.]

4. I go <u>only</u> to the beach on Saturdays. [one place]

   I go to the beach <u>only</u> on Saturdays. [one day per week]

5. He <u>simply</u> hated living. [He absolutely hated living.]

   He hated <u>simply</u> living [He hated merely living.]

6. <u>Not</u> all of the information is printed clearly. [Some of the information is difficult to read.]

   All of the information is <u>not</u> printed clearly. [Call for repairs; the printer is on the fritz.]

Answers to Exercise 70: Connecting Modifiers and Headwords

1. The bridge <u>across the river</u> swayed <u>in the wind</u>.
2. The spectators <u>on the shore</u> viewed <u>in disbelief</u>.
3. <u>Mesmerized by the spectacle</u> they watched the drama unfold.
4. <u>In unison</u>, the spectators feared a disaster was certain.
5. <u>Within the hour</u>, the state police arrived <u>to save the day</u>.
6. They closed off the area <u>with roadblocks.</u>
7. Drivers <u>approaching the bridge</u> were asked to stop.
8. Meanwhile, <u>on the bridge,</u> the scene was chaos.

9. Motorists <u>in their cars</u> sat <u>paralyzed with fear</u>.

10. <u>Struggling against the weather</u>, the police managed to rescue everyone.

11. A newspaper reporter, <u>holding her camera</u>, ran <u>to a telephone</u> <u>at a nearby market</u>.

12. <u>Close to exhaustion</u>, she reported the events <u>to her editor</u>.

ANSWERS TO EXERCISE 71: RELOCATING MISPLACED MODIFIERS

1. She realized after the wedding that she had married the wrong man.
2. *The Prince and the Pauper* by Mark Twain is a novel about an exchange of identities.
3. The energy that he was saving for the marathon was used up in the 10-kilometer race.
4. He loaded the bottles and cans, which he planned to leave at the recycling center, into his new Porsche.
5. Using a graph, the manager explained the sales figures to the board members.
6. The replacement door had been painted from top to bottom before it was delivered to my mother.

ANSWERS TO EXERCISE 72: RELOCATING MISPLACED MODIFIERS

1. The people in the audience finally quieted down when they saw the play was about to begin and realized the orchestra had finished tuning up and had begun the overture.
2. Expecting to enjoy the first act very much, they settled into their seats.
3. However, most people were completely baffled, even after watching and listening for twenty minutes and paying close attention to the drama.
4. In fact, because it had nameless characters, no scenery, and a rambling plot that didn't seem to be heading anywhere, the play puzzled even the drama critics.
5. Finally, speaking directly to the audience, one of the three major characters explained what the play was really about.

ANSWERS TO EXERCISE 73: ELIMINATING DANGLING MODIFIERS

Revisions will vary.

1. Most people agree that Buckminster Fuller's geodesic dome, although architecturally unusual, is well designed.
2. As an out-of-state student without a car, Joe had difficulty getting to off-campus cultural events.
3. To build a campfire, one needs kindling.
4. With every step we took upward, the trees became sparser.
5. Because I am an amateur tennis player, my backhand is weaker than my forehand.
6. When you are exiting the train, the station will be on your right.
7. Driving through the Mojave, I found the landscape bleak and oppressive.
8. The air quality will get better if we require auto manufacturers to further improve emission control devices.
9. Using a piece of filter paper, the lab technician dried the ball of sodium as much as possible and then placed it in a dry test tube.
10. Because I missed work for seven days straight, my job was in jeopardy.
11. Having prepared a romantic candlelight dinner, my fiancée unplugged the telephone so we could enjoy the meal without interruption.
12. While running laps at the track each afternoon, I park my car in front of the gym.
13. When I walked into the dentist's office, the sound of the drill made my heartbeat race.

ANSWERS TO EXERCISE 74: LEVEL OF DICTION

There will be some variation in students' answers here. Discussing their ideas of formal diction in class will help you and your students agree on what formal language is. King's "Letter from Birmingham Jail" is formal, in spite of its use of the first person ("I submit that . . ."). A possible revision of his paragraph appears below.

> This distinction is important: Evading or defying the law, as segregationists have done, would lead to anarchy. Anyone who breaks an unjust law must do so openly, accepting the consequences. A person who breaks an unjust law and goes to prison to call attention to an injustice expresses great respect for law.

ANSWERS TO EXERCISE 75: GENERAL AND SPECIFIC; ABSTRACT AND CONCRETE

This exercise might be assigned in connection with 42c, "Letters of Application and Résumés."

    Part-time jobs I have held include waiting tables, landscaping, and selling stereo equipment. Each of these jobs requires strong communications skills. In my most recent position, I sold automobile stereos. My supervisor was impressed with my ability to help customers select components that fit their budgets and preferences. With my proven success in sales—being named Salesperson of the Month three times last year—I believe I am well-qualified for a position in sales management.

ANSWERS TO EXERCISE 76: DENOTATION AND CONNOTATION

This exercise could be used to initiate a discussion of connotation. Because students often misuse the thesaurus, which usually gives no indication of connotations, you might bring this reference work to class and demonstrate its proper use. Sample answers to the exercise appear below.

Negative
Neutral
Favorable

1. deceive
   mislead
   beguile
2. antiquated
   old
   antique
3. egghead
   intellectual
   genius
4. pathetic
   unfortunate
   touching
5. cheap
   inexpensive
   economical
6. blunder
   error
   mistake
7. weird
   unusual
   unique
8. politician
   public servant
   statesman
9. shack
   cabin
   cottage
10. stench
    smell
    scent

11. swipe
    steal
    purloin
12. treason
    rebellion
    uprising
13. destroy
    suppress
    quell

Answers to Exercise 77: Denotation and Connotation

When the students have written all three sentences, they may find it interesting to see what others have written. They can share their examples with one another in small groups or by reading them aloud. You may also duplicate copies for the class or use an overhead projector so that the class can discuss them.

Answers to Exercise 78: Figures of Speech

Some examples appear below. You and your students will be able to find many others.

simile: shone like silver
metaphor: a broad expanse of river was turned to blood
personification: language of this water

Answers to Exercise 79: Figures of Speech

Some sample sentences to get the students started appear below.

1. The child was as small and as carelessly groomed as an old rag doll. [simile]
2. I want to live life to its fullest, the way Pepsi drinkers do. [allusion]
3. The December morning was moody: first bright, then cloudy, then bright again. [personification]
4. As I walked, I saw clouds floating in the sky, their sails unfurled, traveling at several knots. [metaphor]
5. House cats, like tigers, stalk their prey slowly and silently, moving quickly only when it's too late for the catch to get away. [simile]

Answers to Exercise 80: Eliminating Biased Language

1. Implies that women as a group are poor drivers.

2. Suggests that all medical students are male.
3. United States citizens of East Asian descent usually prefer the term Asian Americans.
4. Denigrates people based on class.
5. A person with a disability might see a wheelchair as liberating, not confining.
6. Implies that hairdressing is an occupation associated with a particular sexual preference.
7. Suggests that people from Tennessee (and the South, in general) are "backward," uncivilized.
8. Adult females should be referred to as women, not as girls.
9. Suggests that all doctors have poor handwriting skills.
10. Suggests that people with strong math capabilities possess weak verbal skills.

ANSWERS TO EXERCISE 81: GENDER-NEUTRAL ALTERNATIVES

Answers and comments will vary. These are some examples.

congressman—member of Congress
forefathers—ancestors
men at work—work crews

ANSWERS TO EXERCISES 82-84: GENDER AND LANGUAGE

You may wish to have your students answer the questions in these exercises in group or class discussions.

ANSWERS TO EXERCISE 85: GRAMMATICAL FORMS

(Using *The American Heritage Dictionary*, 3rd ed.)

1. drank, drunk, drinking, drinks
   deified, deified, deifying, deifies
   caroled, caroled, caroling, carols;
   also carolled, carolled, carolling, carols
   drew, drawn, drawing, draws
   rang, rung, ringing, rings
2. canter, command, lord, minister, mother
3. silos, sheep, seeds or seed, mice, scissors (a plural noun used with either singular or plural verb), genetics (a plural noun used with a singular verb), alchemies (no plural given, so it forms regularly)

4. fast, faster, fastest
airy, airier, airiest
good, better, best
mere, no comparative, merest
homey, homier, homiest
unlucky, unluckier, unluckiest
5. bias: transitive, with no phrase
halt: transitive or intransitive, with no phrase
dissatisfy: transitive, with no phrase
die: intransitive, *died of embarrassment* or *sunlight died in west;* transitive, no phrase
turn: transitive, *turn a knob;* intransitive, *wheels turning at a rapid rate*

ANSWERS TO EXERCISE 86: USAGE RESTRICTIONS

1. [note spelling] nonstandard
2. term in architecture, especially church architecture, and in astronomy
3. informal
4. British: truck; more generally, horse-drawn wagon
5. Scottish: church; British: Presbyterian Church of Scotland
6. slang
7. British: a conjunction
8. mathematical
9. British regional term meaning unleavened bread
10. slang

ANSWERS TO EXERCISE 87: RESEARCH CAPABILITIES

1. 1978
2. after George W. G. Ferris, 1859-96
3. 32.064
4. Jósef Teodor Konrad Nalecz Korzeniowski
5. a modern movement in art and literature in which an attempt is made to portray or interpret the workings of the unconscious mind as manifested in dreams: it is characterized by an irrational, non-contextual arrangement of material.

ANSWERS TO EXERCISE 88: HISTORIES OF WORDS

1. **mountebank:** from Italian *monta in banco,* meaning "he stands on the bench"; refers to the bench stood on by hawkers of medicines at medieval fairs.

2. **pyrrhic:** if referring to the meter, from Greek *purrhikhios* a war dance; if referring to the victory, from King Pyrrhos, whose army defeated the Romans in 279 B.C. but was nearly destroyed itself.
3. **pittance:** from Middle English *pitaunce,* a donation to a monastery.
4. **protean:** from Proteus, the Greek sea god who could change shape at will.
5. **gargantuan:** from Gargantua, the gigantic king with enormous appetites in Rabelais' farce *Gargantua and Pantagruel.*
6. **cicerone:** after the famous Roman author Cicero.
7. **fathom:** from Middle English *fathme,* meaning "outstretched arms."
8. **gossamer:** from Middle English *gos* and *somer,* referring to the softness of goose feathers plucked in summertime.
9. **rigmarole:** from Middle English *rageman rolle,* a scroll used in a game of chance.
10. **maudlin:** corruption of Magdalen as in Mary Magdalen, who was often portrayed in Middle English literature as a weeping penitent.

ANSWERS TO EXERCISE 89: PERIODS

1. Students are sometimes confused by the difference between B.C.E. and C.E.
2. Having gone through rigorous training, they were prepared now for their work in the Peace Corps.
3. correct
4. After she graduated from USC with a J.D., she interviewed with the FBI.
5. The President's press conference at DOE was scheduled for 10 a.m., but it was postponed until 2 p.m.

ANSWERS TO EXERCISE 90: QUESTION MARKS

1. He wondered whether he should take a nine o'clock class.
2. The instructor asked, "Was the Spanish-American War a victory for America?"
3. Are they really going to China?
4. He took a somewhat less than modest portion of dessert—half a pie.
5. "Is *data* the plural of *datum?*" he inquired.

ANSWERS TO EXERCISE 91: EXCLAMATION POINTS

1. Are you kidding? I never said that!
2. When the cell divided, each of the daughter cells had an extra chromosome.
3. This is fantastic! I can't believe you bought this for me!
4. Wow! Just what I always wanted! A pink Cadillac!
5. "Eureka!" cried Archimedes as he sprang from his bathtub.

ANSWERS TO EXERCISE 92: REVIEW OF END PUNCTUATION

Dr. Craig and his group of divers paused at the shore, staring respectfully at the enormous lake. Who could imagine what terrors lay beneath its surface? Which of them might not emerge alive from this adventure? Would it be Col. Cathcart? Capt. Wilks, the M.D. from the naval base? Her husband, P. L. Fox? Or would they all survive the task ahead? Dr. Craig decided some encouraging remarks were in order.

"Attention, divers!" he said in a loud, forceful voice. "May I please have your attention? The project which we are about to undertake—"

"Oh, no!" screamed Mr. Fox suddenly. "Look out! It's the Loch Ness Monster!"

"Quick!" shouted Dr. Craig. "Move away from the shore!" But his warning came too late.

ANSWERS TO EXERCISE 93: COMMAS IN COMPOUND SENTENCES

1. Cross-country skiing was not her favorite activity, nor did she enjoy downhill skiing.
2. Managed health care plans are less expensive than traditional fee-for-service plans, so more employers are including them in the employee benefit package.
3. For their 50th anniversary her parents were considering a trip to Indonesia, or they might take a cruise around the Greek Isles.
4. Mt. Lemon is a ski area near Tucson, Arizona, but most visitors to Tucson come to enjoy the desert sun.
5. Viatical insurance plans may be advantageous for people who are seriously ill, and they may be lucrative financially for those who buy them from ill people.

ANSWERS TO EXERCISE 94: COMMAS TO SEPARATE ITEMS IN A SERIES

1. Cholla, teddy bear, prickly pear, and saguaro are all cacti.
2. The National Park System is responsible for maintaining our national heritage, safeguarding wildlife, and providing positive visitor experiences.
3. The Grand Canyon is in Arizona, but Sequoia, Yosemite, and Death Valley are in California, and Rocky Mountain and Mesa Verde National Parks are in Colorado.
4. Glacier, Yosemite, Yellowstone, Grand Canyon, Great Smoky Mountains, and Grand Tetons are all magnificent parks in the United States.
5. correct

ANSWERS TO EXERCISE 95: COMMAS TO SEPARATE COORDINATE ADJECTIVES

1. rumbling, threatening distant thunder
2. battered, tarnished silver spoon
3. contentious, competitive New York Yankees
4. challenging, exciting miniature golf
5. controversial, innovative Rolling Stones
6. devoted, romantic loving couple
7. modern, innovative computer science
8. natural, nutritious wheat bread
9. freshly painted, dimly lit art museum
10. confusing, frustrating new math

ANSWERS TO EXERCISE 96: COMMAS TO SET OFF INTRODUCTORY ELEMENTS

When the most sagacious of Victorian culinarians, Mrs. Beeton, spoke rather cryptically of the "alliaceous tribe," she was referring to none other than the ancient and noble members of the lily family known in kitchens round the world as the onion, scallion, leek, shallot, clove, and garlic. I don't suppose it really matters that many cooks today are hardly aware of the close affinity the common bulb onion we take so much for granted has with those other vegetables of the *Allium* genus, but it does bother me how Americas underestimate the versatility of the onion and how so few give a second thought to exploiting the potential of its aromatic relatives. More often than not, the onion itself is considered no more than a flavoring agent to soups, stews, stocks, sauces, salads, and sandwiches. Though I'd be the last to deny that nothing awakens the gustatory senses or inspires the soul like the aroma of onions simmering in a lusty stew or the crunch of a few sweet, odoriferous slices on a juicy hamburger, it would be nice to see the onion highlighted in ways other than the all-too-familiar fried rings and creamed preparations.

ANSWERS TO EXERCISE 97: COMMAS TO SET OFF NONRESTRICTIVE ELEMENTS

The Statue of Liberty, which was dedicated in 1886, had undergone extensive renovation. Its supporting structure, whose designer was the French engineer Alexandre Gustave Eiffel, is made of iron. The Statue of Liberty, created over a period of nine years by sculptor Frédéric-August Bartholdi, stands 151 feet tall. The people of France, who were grateful for American help in the French Revolution, raised the money to pay the sculptor who created the statue. The people of the United States, contributing over $100,000, raised the money for the pedestal on which the statue stands.

ANSWERS TO EXERCISE 98: COMMAS TO SET OFF NONESSENTIAL ELEMENTS

1. Kermit the Frog is a muppet, a cross between a marionette and a puppet.
2. The common cold, a virus, is frequently spread by hand contact, not by mouth.
3. correct
4. correct
5. The submarine *Nautilus* was the first to cross under the North Pole, wasn't it?
6. correct
7. Superman was called Kal-El on the planet Krypton; on earth, however, he was known as Clark Kent, not Kal-El.
8. Its sales topping any of his previous singles, "Heartbreak Hotel" was Elvis Presley's first million seller.
9. Two companies, Nash and Hudson, joined in 1954 to form American Motors.
10. A firefly is a beetle, not a fly, and a prairie dog is a rodent, not a dog.

ANSWERS TO EXERCISE 99: COMMAS TO SET OFF QUOTATIONS, NAMES, DATES, ETC.

1. India became independent on August 15, 1947.
2. The UAW has more than 1,500,000 dues-paying members.
3. Nikita Khrushchev, former Soviet premier, said, "We will bury you!"
4. Mount St. Helens, northeast of Portland, Oregon, began erupting on March 27, 1980, and eventually killed at least thirty people.
5. Located at 1600 Pennsylvania Avenue, Washington, D.C., the White House is a major tourist attraction.
6. In 1956, playing before a crowd of 64,519 fans in Yankee Stadium in New York, New York, Don Larsen pitched the first perfect game in World Series history.
7. Lewis Thomas, M.D., was born in Flushing, New York, and attended Harvard Medical School in Cambridge, Massachusetts.
8. In 1967, 2,000,000 people died of smallpox, but in 1977, only about twenty died.
9. "The reports of my death," Mark Twain remarked, "have been greatly exaggerated."
10. The French explorer Jean Nicolet landed at Green Bay, Wisconsin, in 1634, and in 1848, Wisconsin became the thirtieth state; it has 10,355 lakes and a population of more than 4,700,000.

ANSWERS TO EXERCISE 100: COMMAS TO PREVENT MISREADING

1. According to Mitsuoko, Kim's spoken English is excellent.
2. correct
3. By talking, passengers might control their fear of flying.
4. My mother always tells me, "When driving, drive safely."
5. Our airline snack consisted of a stale bun with dry meat, and flavorless cookies.

ANSWERS TO EXERCISE 101: REVIEW OF COMMAS

1. Sometimes they did go shopping or to a movie, but sometimes they went across the highway, ducking fast across the busy road, to a drive-in restaurant where older kids hung out. The restaurant was shaped like a big bottle, though squatter than a real bottle, and on its cap was a revolving figure of a grinning boy who held a hamburger aloft.

2. His head whirled as he stepped into the thronged corridor, and he sank back into one of the chairs against the wall to get his breath. The lights, the chatter, the perfumes, the bewildering medley of color—he had, for a moment, the feeling of not being able to stand it.
3. It has been longed for, campaigned for, kissed and caressed on the top of its shiny, 24-karat-gold-plated bald head. It has inspired giddiness, wordiness, speechlessness, glee, and—in the case of the stars it has eluded—reactions ranging from wonder to rage.
4. Yes, society often did treat the elderly abysmally . . . they were sometimes ignored, sometimes victimized, sometimes poor and frightened, but so many of them were survivors.
5. The word success comes from the Latin verb *succedere,* meaning "to follow after."
6. It was a big, squarish frame house that had once been white, decorated with cupolas and spires and scrolled balconies in the heavily lightsome style of the seventies, set on what had once been our most select street.
7. The world, as always, is debating the issues of war and peace.
8. About fifteen miles below Monterey, on the wild coast, the Torres family had their farm, a few sloping acres above a cliff that dropped to the brown reefs and to the hissing white waters of the ocean.
9. I was looking for myself and asking everyone except myself questions which I, and only I, could answer.
10. According to the Pet Food Institute, a Washington-based trade association, there were about 18 million more dogs than cats in the United States as recently as a decade ago, but today there are 56 million cats and only 52 million dogs.

ANSWERS TO EXERCISE 102: PUNCTUATION TO SEPARATE INDEPENDENT CLAUSES

During the 1950s, movie attendance declined because of the increasing popularity of television. As a result, numerous gimmicks were introduced to draw audiences into theaters. One of the first of these was Cinerama. In this technique three pictures were shot side by side and projected on a curved screen. Next came 3-D, complete with special glasses; *Bwana Devil* and *The Creature from the Black Lagoon* were two early 3-D ventures. *The Robe* was the first picture filmed in Cinemascope; in this technique a shrunken image was projected on a screen twice as wide as it was tall. Smell-O-Vision (or Aroma-rama) was a short-lived gimmick that enabled audiences to smell what they were viewing, but problems developed when it became impossible to get one odor out of the theater in time for the next smell to be introduced. William Castle's *Thirteen Ghosts* introduced special glasses for cowardly viewers who wanted to be able to control what they saw; the red part of the glasses was the "ghost viewer," and the green part was the "ghost remover." Perhaps the ultimate in movie gimmicks accompanied the film *The Tingler*. When this film was shown, seats in the theater were wired to generate mild electric shocks. Unfortunately, the shocks set off a chain reaction that led to hysteria in the theater. During the 1960s, such gimmicks all but disappeared, and viewers were able once again to simply sit back and enjoy a movie.

ANSWERS TO EXERCISE 103: SEMICOLONS TO SEPARATE INDEPENDENT CLAUSES

1. Television soap operas provide a diversion to real life; soap opera characters are always wealthy and never seem to work.
2. Ads on afternoon soap operas are directed primarily at women and rarely at men; these ads for women include soap, toothpaste, skin creams, and nail products.
3. Hale-Bopp was an extraordinary comet seen by millions of ordinary people; it was visible at sunrise and sunset in the spring of 1997 throughout the United States.
4. In many places in the United States, the legal system finds it difficult to try rape cases; victims feel shame and are embarrassed to testify.
5. I looked for a long time for an article on babies born addicted to cocaine; the article was hard to find, but it was quite useful.
6. On the bottom of the shelf sits an almost obsolete, yet once expensive, turntable, a dusty 8-track player, and large speakers; across the room in a prominent position on the entertainment center resides a gleaming CD player.
7. The United States Capitol is at one end of the Mall with the Washington Monument at the other; the space in-between is used by both visitors and residents for volleyball, sunbathing, and strolling.

ANSWERS TO EXERCISE 104: SENTENCE COMBINING

1. Teachers will instruct students on differences between formal and casual language and will give writing assignments requiring formal language; however, the purpose is not to destroy the language which students use.

2. The purpose is to make students more versatile in language use; for example, students should be able to do essay tests, short answer tests, and full-length compositions as well as professional writing such as résumés and job applications.
3. Some students think that the whole idea is silly, and talking about language is a waste of time; still, sixteen-year-old Marta Sharif said they could use some lessons in language courtesy.
4. Marta continued, saying she gets tired of hearing foul language; unfortunately, she said that she hears this language frequently as she walks across campus.

or

Marta continued, saying she gets tired of hearing foul language; she said that, unfortunately, she hears this language frequently as she walks across campus.
5. Her parents are appalled at the language they hear from young people in public and support the school's efforts; in fact, they would like to see the efforts go further.

ANSWERS TO EXERCISE 105: SEMICOLONS TO SEPARATE ITEMS IN A SERIES

1. Margaret Atwood wrote *Lady Oracle*, which is about the life crisis of a middle-aged woman; *The Robber Bride*, which tells the intricate, age-old story of women and men; and *Alias Grace*, which is a fictionalized account of a real-life, nineteenth-century murder.
2. A new, inexpensive automobile has several advantages for a college student: the monthly payments will be low, which is especially important for the budget; it won't require costly repairs, which usually are needed at the worst possible moment; and, after graduation, it can be used as a down payment on a newer model.
3. Properly prescribed antidepressants, such as Prozac and Paxil, may benefit the patient by easing anxiety, therefore allowing the person to concentrate better; by improving sleep patterns, which is especially important for people who must mentally focus on important tasks; and by moderating the sometimes severe blue moods of depression.
4. Both high school and college students may use the term "geek" to describe an extremely bright, socially unskilled person; "nerd" to describe someone neither bright, socially skilled, nor well-dressed; and "jock" to describe the muscular, athletic, usually non-academically oriented student.

5. The process of registering for college is often a hassle, requiring a student to stand seemingly for hours in long, curving lines; to fill out endless, meaningless forms; and to walk from building to building in search of the right advisor to sign those forms.

ANSWERS TO EXERCISE 106: SENTENCE COMBINING

1. A good dictionary offers definitions of words, including some obsolete and nonstandard words; provides information about synonyms, usage, and word origins; and also offers information on pronunciation and syllabication.
2. The flags of the Scandinavian countries all depict a cross on a solid background: Denmark's flag is red with a white cross; Norway's flag is also red, but its cross is blue, outlined in white; and Sweden's flag is blue with a yellow cross.
3. Over one hundred international collectors' clubs are thriving today, including the Cola Clan, whose members buy, sell, and trade Coca-Cola memorabilia; the Cirtus Label Society; and a Cookie Cutter Collectors' Club.
4. Listening to the radio special, we heard "Shuffle Off to Buffalo" and "Moon over Miami," both of which are about eastern cities; "By the Time I Get to Phoenix" and "I Left My Heart in San Francisco," which mention western cities; and finally "The Star-Spangled Banner," which seemed to be an appropriate finale.
5. There are three principal types of contact lenses: hard contact lenses, also called conventional lenses, which are easy to clean and handle and are quite sturdy; less durable soft lenses, which are easily contaminated and must be cleaned and disinfected daily; and gas-permeable lenses, which look and feel like hard lenses but are more easily contaminated and less durable.

ANSWERS TO EXERCISE 107: REVIEW OF SEMICOLONS

Barnstormers were aviators who toured the country after World War I, giving people short airplane rides and exhibitions of stunt flying; in fact, the name *barnstormer* was derived from the use of barns as airplane hangars. Americans' interest in airplanes had all but disappeared after the war; planes had served their function in battle, but when the war ended, most people saw no future in aviation. The barnstormers helped popularize flying, especially in rural areas. Some of them were pilots who had flown in the war; others were just young men with a thirst for adventure. They gave people rides in airplanes, sometimes charging a dollar a minute. For most passengers, this was their first ride in an airplane; in fact, sometimes it was their first sight of one. In the early 1920s people grew bored with what the barnstormers had to offer, so groups of pilots began to stage spectacular—but often dangerous—stunt shows. Then, after Lindbergh's 1927 flight across the Atlantic, Americans suddenly needed no encouragement to embrace aviation. The barnstormers had outlived their usefulness, and an era ended.

ANSWERS TO EXERCISE 108: POSSESSIVES

1. American Airlines' flights
2. the attorney's briefs
3. Mrs. Irie's children
4. Janna Deppas's classes
    or
    Janna Deppas' classes
5. Ricardo Ortiz's speech
6. Nicole Baday's iguanas
7. Mulu Menshu's sweater
8. Judy and her husband's nanny
9. Thomas Jefferson's unique designs
10. the President's supporters' dinner

ANSWERS TO EXERCISE 109: POSSESSIVES

1. Delta Airlines' routes are worldwide.
2. John Adam's contributions to the transition of the United States from colony to self-government are sometimes under appreciated.
    or
    John Adams' contributions to the transition of the United States from colony to self-government are sometimes under appreciated.
3. Stephen King's and Danielle Steel's novels are perfect for summer vacation reading.
4. Phoenix's Desert Museum highlights visitors' sightseeing excursions.
5. T.V.'s graphic violence and sex are under scrutiny by politicians and the public.

ANSWERS TO EXERCISE 110: PLURAL NOUNS OR POSSESSIVE PRONOUNS

1. Ours are the ones you should be careful about.
2. Pacific Airlines' seats seem adequate primarily for smaller passengers.
3. My parents' seats on Pacific Airlines are two rows behind yours.

4. The popularity of cable television challenges the three major networks' profits.
5. Potato chips and soft drinks are a standard diet of hers.
6. Flight attendants' jobs are often hectic.
7. Many passengers ignore safety regulations at the beginning of flights.
8. Geena Davis's role in *Earth Girls Are Easy* strengthened her acting credentials.

    or

    Geena Davis' role in *Earth Girls Are Easy* strengthened her acting credentials.
9. *The Firm,* John Grisham's novel, was made into a successful movie, as were several of his other books.
10. correct

ANSWERS TO EXERCISE 111: CONTRACTIONS

1. Whose movies do you think are better: Delta's or American's?
2. The pilot turned on the seat belt sign because it's a rough flight.
3. If it's much rougher, you're going to spill your coffee.
4. They're trying to read the newspaper, but they're finding the airplane too bouncy.
5. Occasionally, you're going to find it too rough even to hold your soft drink can without its spilling.
6. correct
7. "Ours is the flight to Taiwan," I said.
8. Having seen their hard work, I like to thank the flight attendants personally.
9. The special lunches were ours, but they were given to others.
10. Our landing at Heathrow Airport was smooth, but there was no gate agent to meet us.

ANSWERS TO EXERCISE 112: PLURALS OF LETTERS AND NUMBERS

1. In the game of tic-tac-toe, players line up *X*'s and *O*'s to win.
2. "They said they were goin' to school, but I think they were just playin' hooky!"
3. His writing incorporated many *prioritize's, parameter's,* and *indicator's.*
4. When I write 7's in the United States, they look different from my 7's when I'm in France; the same is true for *Z*'s.

    or

    When I write 7s in the United States, they look different from my 7s when I'm in France; the same is true for Zs.

5. Most faculty have multiple degrees including M.A.'s, M.S.'s, and M.F.A.'s.

Answers to Exercise 113: Direct Quotations

1. Mr. Fox noted, "Few people can explain what Descartes' words 'I think, therefore I am' actually mean."
2. Gertrude Stein said, "You are all a lost generation."
3. "Freedom of speech does not guarantee anyone the right to yell 'Fire!' in a crowded theater," she explained.
4. correct
5. "If everyone will sit down," the teacher announced, "the exam will begin."

Answers to Exercise 114: Titles and Words Used in a Special Sense

1. "First Fig" and "Second Fig" are two of the poems in Edna St. Vincent Millay's *Collected Poems*.
2. In the article "Feminism Takes a New Turn," Betty Friedan reconsiders some of the issues first raised in her 1964 book *The Feminine Mystique*.
3. Edwin Arlington Robinson's poem "Richard Cory" was the basis for the song "Richard Cory" recorded by Paul Simon.
4. *Beside* means "next to," but *besides* means "except."
5. In an essay on the novel *An American Tragedy* published in *The Yale Review*, Robert Penn Warren noted, "Theodore Dreiser once said that his philosophy of love might be called 'Varietism.'"

Answers to Exercise 115: Dialogue

The next time, the priest steered me into the confession box himself and left the shutter back [so] I could see him get in and sit down at the further side of the grille from me.
"Well, now," he said, "what do they call you?"
"Jackie, father," said I.
"And what's a-trouble to you, Jackie?"
"Father," said I, feeling I might as well get it over while I had him in good humor, "I had it all arranged to kill my grandmother."
He seemed a bit shaken by that, all right, because he said nothing for quite a while.
"My goodness," he said at last, "that'd be a shocking thing to do. What put that into your head?"

"Father," I said, feeling very sorry for myself, "she's an awful woman."

"Is she?" he asked. "What way is she awful?"

"She takes porter, father," I said, knowing well from the way Mother talked of it that this was a mortal sin, and hoping it would make the priest take a more favorable view of my case.

"Oh, my!" he said, and I could see that he was impressed.

"And snuff, father," said I.

"That's a bad case, sure enough, Jackie," he said.

ANSWERS TO EXERCISE 116: REVIEW OF QUOTATION MARKS

In her essay "The Obligation to Endure" from the book *Silent Spring*, Rachel Carson writes: "As Albert Schweitzer has said, 'Man can hardly even recognize the devils of his own creation.'" Carson goes on to point out that many chemicals have been used to kill insects and other organisms which, she writes, are "described in the modern vernacular as 'pests.'" Carson believes such supposedly advanced chemicals, by contaminating our environment, do more harm than good. In addition to *Silent Spring*, Carson is also the author of the book *The Sea Around Us*. This work, divided into three sections ("Mother Sea," "The Restless Sea," and "Man and the Sea about Him"), was first published in 1951.

ANSWERS TO EXERCISE 117: REVIEW OF QUOTATION MARKS

1. "Kilroy was here" and "Women and children first" are two expressions *Bartlett's Familiar Quotations* attributes to Anon.
2. Correct; indirect quotation
3. "The answer, my friend," Bob Dylan sang, "is blowin' in the wind."
4. The novel was a real thriller, complete with spies and counter-spies, mysterious women, and exotic international chases.
5. The sign said, "Road liable to subsidence"; it meant that we should look out for potholes.
6. One of William Blake's best-known lines—"To see a world in a grain of sand"—opens his poem "Auguries of Innocence."
7. In James Thurber's short story "The Catbird Seat," Mrs. Barrows annoys Mr. Martin by asking silly questions like "Are you tearing up the pea patch?" "Are you scraping the bottom of the pickle barrel?" and "Are you lifting the oxcart out of the ditch?"
8. "I'll make him an offer he can't refuse," promised the godfather in Mario Puzo's novel.
9. What did Timothy Leary mean by "Turn on, tune in, drop out"?

10. George, the protagonist of Bernard Malamud's short story "A Summer's Reading" is something of an underachiever.

ANSWERS TO EXERCISE 118: COLONS

1. Books about the late John F. Kennedy include the following: *A Hero for Our Time; Johnny, We Hardly Knew Ye; One Brief Shining Moment;* and *JFK: Reckless Youth.*
2. Only one task remained: to tell his boss he was quitting.
3. The story closed with a familiar phrase: "And they all lived happily ever after."
4. The sergeant requested [delete colon] reinforcements, medical supplies, and more ammunition.
5. She kept only four souvenirs: a photograph, a matchbook, a theater program, and a daisy pressed between the pages of *William Shakespeare: The Complete Works.*

ANSWERS TO EXERCISE 119: DASHES

1. Tulips, daffodils, hyacinths, lilies—all of these flowers grow from bulbs.
2. St. Kitts and Nevis—two tiny island nations—are now independent after 360 years of British rule.
3. "But it's not—" She paused and reconsidered her next words.
4. He considered several different majors—history, English, political science, and business—before deciding on journalism.
5. The two words added to the Pledge of Allegiance in the 1950s—"under God"—remain part of the Pledge today.

ANSWERS TO EXERCISE 120: PARENTHESES

1. George Orwell's *1984* (1949) focuses on the dangers of a totalitarian society.
2. The final score (45-0) was a devastating blow for the Eagles.
3. Belize (formerly British Honduras) is a country in Central America.
4. The first phonics book *(Phonics Is Fun)* has a light blue cover.
5. Some high school students have so many extracurricular activities (band, sports, drama club, and school newspaper, for instance) that they have little time to study.

ANSWERS TO EXERCISE 121: ELLIPSES

Answers will vary. Some possibilities appear below. This is a good exercise to discuss in connection with a research paper assignment.

Students must determine what information is essential here and must be prepared to explain their choices. An additional instruction might incorporate part of the quotation into a hypothetical research paper paragraph.

1. "When I was eighteen . . . my mother told me that when out with a young man I should always leave a half-hour before I wanted to."
2. "When I was eighteen or thereabouts, my mother told me that when out with a young man I should always leave a half-hour before I wanted to. . . . I recognized this advice as sound, and exactly the same rule applies to research."
3. "One must stop *before* one has finished. . . ."
4. "The most important thing about research is to know when to stop. . . . When I was eighteen or thereabouts, my mother told me that when out with a young man I should always leave a half-hour before I wanted to."

ANSWERS TO EXERCISE 122: REVIEW OF COLONS, DASHES, PARENTHESES, BRACKETS, SLASHES

1. Mark Twain (Samuel L. Clemens) made the following statement: "I can live for two months on a good compliment."
2. Liza Minelli, the actress/singer who starred in several films, is the daughter of Judy Garland. For emphasis, dashes may replace the commas.
3. Saudi Arabia, Oman, Yemen, Qatar, and the United Arab Emirates —all these are located on the Arabian Peninsula.
4. John Adams (1735-1826) was the second president of the United States; John Quincy Adams (1767-1848) was the sixth.
5. The sign said, "No tresspassing [*sic*]."
6. *Checkmate*—a term derived from the Persian phrase meaning "the king is dead"—announces victory in chess. (Parentheses are another option.)
7. The following people were present at the meeting: the president of the board of trustees, three trustees, and twenty reporters.
8. Before the introduction of the potato in Europe, the parsnip was a major source of carbohydrates—in fact, it was a dietary staple.
9. In this well-researched book (*Crime Movies* [New York: Norton 1980]), Carlos Clarens studies the gangster genre in film.
10. I remember reading—though I can't remember where—that Upton Sinclair sold plots to Jack London.

Answers to Exercise 123: *ie* or *ei*

1. receipt
2. variety
3. caffeine
4. achieve
5. kaleidoscope
6. mischief
7. efficient
8. vein
9. species
10. sufficient

Answers to Exercise 124: Suffixes

1. surprising
2. surely
3. forcible
4. manageable
5. duly
6. outrageous
7. serviceable
8. awful
9. shaming
10. shameless

Answers to Exercise 125: Final *y*

1. journeying
2. studied
3. carrying
4. shyly
5. studying
6. sturdiness
7. merriment
8. likelihood
9. plentiful
10. supplier

Answers to Exercise 126: Capitalization

1. The Brontë sisters wrote *Jane Eyre* and *Wuthering Heights,* two nineteenth-century novels that are required reading in many English classes that study Victorian literature.
2. It was a beautiful day in the spring—it was April 15, to be exact—but all Ted could think about was the check he had to write to the Internal Revenue Service and the bills he had to pay by Friday.
3. Traveling north, they hiked through British Columbia, planning a leisurely return on the cruise ship *Canadian Princess.*
4. Alice liked her mom's apple pie better than Aunt Nellie's rhubarb pie; but she liked Grandpa's punch best of all.
5. A new elective, Political Science 30, covers the Vietnam War from the Gulf of Tonkin to the fall of Saigon, including the roles of Ho Chi Minh, the Viet Cong, and the Buddhist monks; the positions of Presidents Johnson and Nixon; and the influence of groups like the Student Mobilization Committee and Vietnam Veterans Against the War.

6. When the Central High School Drama Club put on a production of Shaw's *Pygmalion*, the director xeroxed extra copies of the parts for Eliza Doolittle and Professor Henry Higgins so he could give them to the understudies.
7. Shaking all over, Bill admitted, "Driving on the Los Angeles Freeway is a frightening experience for a kid from the Bronx, even in a BMW."
8. The new United Federation of Teachers contract guarantees teachers many paid holidays, including Columbus Day, Veterans Day, and Washington's Birthday; a week each at Christmas and Easter; and two full months (July and August) in the summer.
9. The sociology syllabus included the books *Beyond the Best Interests of the Child*, *Regulating the Poor*, and *A Welfare Mother*; in anthropology we were to begin by studying the Stone Age; and in geology we were to focus on the Mesozoic Era.
10. Winners of the Nobel Peace Prize include Lech Walesa, former leader of the Polish trade union Solidarity; the Reverend Dr. Martin Luther King, Jr., founder of the Southern Christian Leadership Conference; and Bishop Desmond Tutu of South Africa.

ANSWERS TO EXERCISE 127: ITALICS

1. I said *Carol* not *Darryl*.
2. A *deus ex machina*, an improbable device used to resolve the plot of a fictional work, is used in Charles Dickens's novel *Oliver Twist*.
3. He dotted every *i* and crossed every *t*.
4. The Metropolitan Opera's production of *Carmen* was a *tour de force* for the principal performers.
5. correct
6. *Antidote* and *anecdote* are often confused because their pronunciations are similar.
7. Hawthorne's novels include *Fanshawe*, *The House of the Seven Gables*, *The Blithedale Romance*, and *The Scarlet Letter*.
8. Words like *mailman*, *policeman*, and *fireman* are rapidly being replaced by nonsexist terms like *letter carrier*, *police officer*, and *firefighter*.
9. A classic black tuxedo was considered *de rigueur* at the charity ball, but Jason preferred to wear his *dashiki*.
10. Thomas Mann's novel *Buddenbrooks* is a *Bildungsroman*.

Answers to Exercise 128: Hyphens

1. tran/scen/den/tal/ism
   tran-scendentalism or transcen-dentalism
2. cal/li/o/pe
   calli-ope
3. mar/tyr
   mar-tyr
4. lon/gi/tude
   longi-tude
5. book/keep/er
   book-keeper
6. side-/split/ting
   side-splitting
7. mark/ed/ly
   markedly [no break]
8. a/maz/ing
   amaz-ing
9. un/like/ly
   un-likely
10. thor/ough
    thor-ough

Answers to Exercise 129: Hyphens

1. long-lost relative
2. video-game addict
3. door-to-door salesman
4. eye-catching display
5. dearly beloved friends
6. child-centered household
7. hard-to-follow line of reasoning
8. New York-New Jersey border
9. thirty-two-year-old candidate
10. user-friendly computer

Answers to Exercise 130: Hyphens

1. One of the restaurant's blue-plate specials is chicken-fried steak.
2. Virginia and Texas are both right-to-work states.
3. He stood on tiptoe to see the near-perfect statue, which was well hidden by the security fence.
4. The five- and ten-cent store had a self-service make-up counter and many up-to-the-minute gadgets.

5. The so-called Saturday night special is opposed by pro-gun-control groups.
6. He ordered two all-beef patties with special sauce, lettuce, cheese, pickles, and onions on a sesame seed bun.
7. The material was extremely thought provoking, but it hardly presented any earth-shattering conclusions.
8. The Dodgers-Phillies game was rained out, so the long-suffering fans left for home.
9. Bone-marrow transplants carry the risk of what is known as a graft-versus-host reaction.
10. The state-funded child care program was considered a highly desirable alternative to family day care.

ANSWERS TO EXERCISE 131: ABBREVIATIONS

1. The committee meeting, attended by representatives from Action for Children's Television (ACT) and the National Organization for Women (NOW), Senator Putnam, and the president of ABC, convened at 8 A.M. on Monday, February 24, at the YWCA on Germantown Avenue.
2. An economics professor was suspended after he encouraged his students to speculate on securities issued by corporations under investigation by the Securities and Exchange Commission (SEC).
3. Benjamin Spock, the M.D. who wrote *Baby and Child Care*, is a respected doctor known throughout the USA.
4. [If this sentence can be defined as "technical writing" (see 35b).]
5. The Reverend Dr. Martin Luther King, Jr., leader of the Southern Christian Leadership Conference (SCLC), led the famous Selma, Alabama, march.
6. William Golding, a novelist from the United Kingdom, won the Nobel Prize in literature.
7. The adult education center, financed by a major computer corporation, offers courses in basic subjects like introductory biology and technical writing as well as teaching programming languages such as PASCAL.
8. All the brothers in the fraternity agreed to write to President Dexter appealing their disciplinary probation under Chapter 4, Section 3 of the Inter-Fraternity Council constitution.
9. A four-quart (that is, one-gallon) container is needed to hold the salt solution.
10. According to Professor Morrison all those taking the MCATs should bring two sharpened no. 2 pencils to the St. Joseph's University auditorium on Saturday.

ANSWERS TO EXERCISE 132: NUMBERS

1. correct (*1984* is a book title.)
2. correct
3. In a control group of 247 patients, almost 3 out of 4 suffered serious adverse reactions to the new drug.
4. Before the Thirteenth Amendment to the Constitution, slaves were counted as three-fifths of a person.
5. The intensive membership drive netted 2,608 new members and additional dues of over five thousand dollars.
6. They had only two choices: Either they could take the yacht at Pier 14, or they could return home to the penthouse at 27 Harbor View Drive.
7. correct
8. Approximately 300,000 schoolchildren in District 6 were given hearing and vision examinations between May 3 and June 26.
9. The United States was drawn into World War II by the Japanese attack on Pearl Harbor on December 7, 1941.
10. An upper-middle-class family can spend over 250,000 dollars to raise each child up to age eighteen.

ANSWERS TO EXERCISE 133: TIME MANAGEMENT

Students may need your help to establish a reasonable research schedule that promotes steady work rather than a mad rush the night before the due date.

ANSWERS TO EXERCISE 134: DISCOVERING YOUR RESEARCH QUESTION

You might ask students to complete this exercise before or during a conference with you.

ANSWERS TO EXERCISE 135: EXPLORING YOUR TOPIC AND LOCATING SOURCES

You may need to advise students on the feasibility of keeping these reference lists on their computers.

ANSWERS TO EXERCISE 136: EVALUATING SOURCES

You might provide a suitable article for students to work with, or you might want them to choose an article related to a subject they are writing about.

Answers to Exercise 137: Locating and Evaluating Sources on the Web Using URL's

Answers will vary.

Answers to Exercise 138: Locating and Evaluating Sources on the Web Using a Key Word Search

Answers will vary.

Answers to Exercise 139: Doing Your Own Key Word Search

Answers will vary.

Answers to Exercise 140: Citing Electronic Sources

Answers will vary. Refer your students to the Documentation section of *The* Brief *Holt Handbook.*

(For Exercises 141-144, you may want students to work with source material they have located instead of or in addition to the Jones passage.)

Answers to Exercise 141: Summarizing

Answers will vary. One sample of each activity follows.

Summary

The movement of people into the suburbs was the largest resettlement in United States history. From 1950 to 1970 the number of people living in the suburbs doubled, and the national mobility rate increased.

To accommodate these people, homebuilders turned farmlands into developments of three-bedroom houses owned by young couples holding government loans. By 1960, the percentage of homeowners had risen above that of renters; most homeowners now lived in the new suburbs.

Abraham Levitt built the three largest suburbs. The first Levittown had 17,447 identical houses, occupied by couples who either had or wanted to have children.

Answers to Numbered Exercises

Answers to Exercise 142: Paraphrasing

Paraphrase (Paragraph 3)

The suburbs became "gigantic nurseries." Abraham Levitt, the son of Russian-Jewish immigrants and the builder of military barracks in World War II, constructed the largest developments. A Long Island potato field became the first Levittown, which housed 82,000 people in 17,447 homes. Two more communities were built on the East Coast. Each offered identical four-room houses with built-in television, outdoor grill, washer, and attic for $7,900, or $60 per month. The common denominator among Levittown residents was the desire to have children.

Answers to Exercise 143: Quoting

Notes (Paragraph 3)

- largest suburban developments, which Jones calls "gigantic nurseries," built by Abraham Levitt
- first Levittown on Long Island; two others on East Coast
- $7,900 or $60 a month for "Monopoly-board bungalow with four rooms, attic, washing machine, outdoor barbecue, and a television set built into the wall"
- 17,447 units/82,000 people/lots of children

Answers to Exercise 144: Documentation

1. Parenthetical citations
   Your students' citations will vary according to the requirements of each paragraph.
2. Works cited entry
   Jones, Landon Y. *Great Expectations: America and the Baby Boom Generation.* New York: Ballantine, 1986.